MARY BERRY'S
HOME COOKING

Macdonald

Editorial manager
Judith Maxwell
Series editor
Neil Tennant
Editor
Linda Sonntag
Designer
Peter Benoist
Production
Susan Mead

© Macdonald Educational Ltd
1980
Text © Thames Television Ltd 1980

Published in association with
Thames Television's programme
After Noon Plus edited by Catherine
Freeman

First published 1980
Macdonald Educational Ltd
Holywell House
Worship St
London EC2A 2EN

ISBN 0 356 06208 2

Contents

Introduction

My third After Noon Plus cookbook is packed with nourishing economical dishes that can be cooked up for the family in no time at all - often from ingredients that are already to hand in a well stocked larder.

The main meals include plenty of traditional favourites using the cheaper cuts of meat as well as several exciting new ways of cooking chicken. For those special occasions why not try English duckling or duck with orange sauce.

As usual during the year my postbag has been full of requests for more cakes, gâteaux and puddings, and this is my opportunity to give you my latest collection of recipes for them. Some are elaborate, others sinfully rich, but all are equally delicious.

The book finishes with a selection of useful standbys that people are always asking my advice on, like jams, chutneys, salad dressings and a basic bread mix.

My thanks go to Clare Blunt who tests all the recipes to make sure they turn out just right, to Rosemary Wadey who prepares the food for photography with such skill, to my editor Linda Sonntag for her care and enthusiasm, and to John Lee for his beautiful camera work. Lastly I'd like to mention my husband Paul and my children Thomas, William and Annabel, who always enjoy home cooking so much.

Mary Berry shopping outside Russell's, New Cavendish Street, London W1.

Soup and good beginnings

Quick cream of tomato soup

2 oz butter
1 large onion, finely
    chopped
2 oz flour
1 pint water
1 pint milk
5 oz can tomato puree
2 teaspoons caster sugar
salt and ground pepper
chopped parsley

50 gm butter
1 large onion, finely
    chopped
50 gm flour
600 ml water
600 ml milk
150 gm can tomato puree
2 teaspoons caster sugar
salt and ground black pepper
chopped parsley

Good onion soup

If you have stock on hand for this recipe, do use it. However, I find that stock cubes are perfectly good enough as the onions give an excellent flavour. When frying the onions cook very slowly, turning frequently so that they become golden brown without catching at the edges. A dark brown or black colour means that the soup will be bitter, so take care.

2 oz good dripping
1 lb onions, finely chopped
1 oz flour
1½ pints water
2 chicken stock cubes
salt and pepper
gravy browning
2 oz grated Cheddar cheese

50 gm good dripping
450 gm onions, finely
    chopped
25 gm flour
900 ml water
2 chicken stock cubes
salt and pepper
gravy browning
50 gm grated Cheddar
    cheese

Melt the dripping in a large pan. Add the onion and fry gently, stirring occasionally until they are beginning to brown. Stir in the flour and cook stirring constantly until the mixture is browned. Gradually add the water and bring to the boil, stirring all the time. Add the stock cubes, seasoning and a little gravy browning to give a good colour. Cover the pan and simmer for 40 minutes. Serve hot sprinkled with cheese. Serves 4.

Melt the butter in a saucepan. Add the onion and fry, stirring occasionally for 5 minutes or until soft but not brown. Stir in the flour and cook for a minute.

Remove the pan from the heat and gradually add the water, return to the heat and bring to the boil, then blend in the milk stirring constantly. Add the puree, sugar and seasoning and simmer the soup for 15 to 20 minutes or until the onion is tender.

Taste and check seasoning and serve hot sprinkled with parsley. Serves 4.

Spinach soup

To make croutons, cut 2 slices of bread ½ inch (1.25 cm) thick and remove crusts and dice. Melt 2 oz (50 gm) butter in a small frying pan and fry the bread slowly until golden brown all over. Drain on kitchen paper and serve in a small bowl.

If you prefer a thicker soup, add a level tablespoon of flour blended with 3 tablespoons of cold stock or water when adding the 1½ pints (900 ml) stock.

2 oz butter
1 small onion, chopped
½ lb frozen leaf spinach
2 chicken stock cubes
1½ pints water
about ¼ level teaspoon salt
pepper
1 tablespoon lemon juice
1 bayleaf
large pinch nutmeg
¼ pint single cream
fried bread croutons

50 gm butter
1 small onion, chopped
225 gm frozen leaf spinach
2 chicken stock cubes
900 ml water
about ¼ level teaspoon salt
pepper
1 tablespoon lemon juice
1 bayleaf
large pinch nutmeg
150 ml single cream
fried bread croutons

Melt the butter in a saucepan, add the onion and fry for 5 minutes or until soft.

Add the spinach, stock cubes, water, seasoning, lemon juice, bayleaf and nutmeg, bring to the boil stirring and then cover the pan and simmer gently for 15 to 20 minutes. Remove the bayleaf and cool the soup.

Reduce to a puree by sieving or put in an electric blender in small amounts and puree. Rinse out the pan, return the soup to it and bring back to the boil. Taste and check seasoning. Just before serving stir in the cream. This soup may also be served chilled in which case, after reducing to a puree and checking seasoning, cool and then chill thoroughly. Before serving stir in the cream.

Serve croutons with the hot soup. Serves 4 to 6.

Soup à la reine

3 oz butter
4 oz onion, chopped
1 large parsnip, cubed
1 clove garlic, crushed
1 oz flour
1 rounded teaspoon curry
  powder
2 pints beef stock
salt and pepper
$\frac{1}{4}$ pint single cream
snipped chives or chopped
  parsley

75 gm butter
100 gm onion, chopped
1 large parsnip, cubed
1 clove garlic, crushed
25 gm flour
1 rounded teaspoon curry
  powder
1.1l beef stock
salt and pepper
150 ml single cream
snipped chives or chopped
  parsley

Melt the butter in a large pan and add the onion, parsnip and garlic and fry gently for 10 minutes. Stir in the flour and curry powder and cook for a minute, then add the stock and seasoning and bring to the boil, stirring. Cover and simmer gently for 20 to 30 minutes or until the parsnip is tender.

Sieve or puree the soup in an electric blender. Rinse out the pan and return the soup. Reheat and taste and check seasoning and when ready to serve, remove from the heat and stir in the cream. Pour into a tureen and sprinkle with chives or parsley. Serves 6.

The large parsnip should be about 1 lb (450 gm) in weight. This is a superb soup, and no one would guess it was based on the humble parsnip.

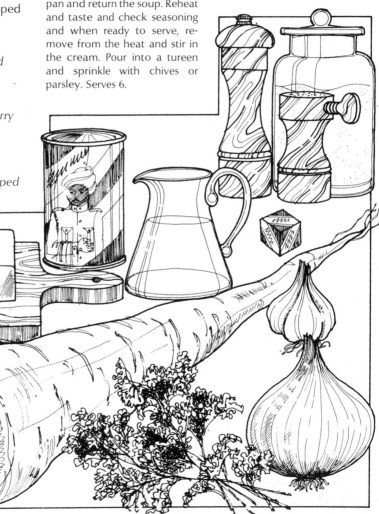

Cook's Tip

Sometimes I use mint jelly instead of mint sauce to flavour this dish, in which case I decrease the sugar and mash the jelly with a fork to blend it with the other dressing ingredients.

1 Honeydew or Galia melon
¾ lb firm tomatoes
1 cucumber
Mint dressing:
about 10 sprigs of mint or 2 teaspoons bought mint sauce concentrate
3 tablespoons caster sugar
2 tablespoons wine vinegar
salt
ground black pepper
6 tablespoons oil

Melon and tomato in mint dressing

Cut the melon in half and remove the seeds. Either scoop the melon flesh out using a melon baller or cut in wedges and then cut the flesh into cubes. Skin and quarter the

1 Honeydew or Galia melon
350 gm firm tomatoes
1 cucumber
Mint dressing:
about 10 sprigs of mint or 2 teaspoons bought mint sauce concentrate
3 tablespoons caster sugar
2 tablespoons wine vinegar
salt
ground black pepper
6 tablespoons oil

tomatoes. Remove the seeds and put on one side (these can be used up in soup or added to a casserole). If the tomatoes are large cut each quarter in half. Peel the cucumber with a potato peeler and cut into neat dice and then put in a large bowl with the melon and tomatoes and mix well together.

To make the dressing: chop the mint very finely with the sugar and place in a screw top jar with the vinegar, salt, pepper and oil and shake well. Pour over the fruit and vegetables and cover and leave in the refrigerator for about 5 hours. Taste and check seasoning and then spoon into 6 glasses and garnish with a sprig of mint. Serve very cold with hot garlic roll or bread (see page 54). Serves 6.

Garlic mushrooms with cream

Cook's Tip

Extremely delicious if you use really fresh snow white button mushrooms.

Wash the mushrooms and trim the ends of the stalks. Melt the butter in a saucepan, add the garlic and mushrooms and cook for 5 minutes. Season well, stir in the cream and simmer gently for a further 5 minutes or until the mushrooms are tender. Serve hot with cheese bread rolls (p.54). Garnish with parsley. Serves 4.

12 oz small button mushrooms
1½ oz butter
1 clove garlic, crushed
salt
freshly ground black pepper
¼ pint double cream

350 gm small button mushrooms
40 gm butter
1 clove garlic, crushed
salt ·
freshly ground black pepper
150 ml double cream

Family meat dishes

Bristol beef casserole

Large Cornish pie

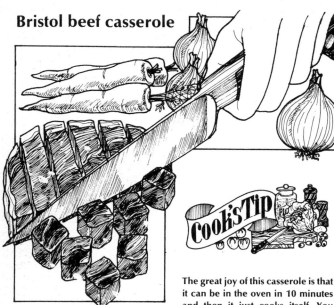

This mixture can be used to make traditional Cornish pasties by cutting a piece of pastry the size of a saucer, placing the meat in the centre and pulling the edges up together at the top, pressing well together and crimping. Cook as for the pie but allow 5 to 10 minutes less.

The great joy of this casserole is that it can be in the oven in 10 minutes and then it just cooks itself. You would never guess the basis was a can of tomato soup.

Cut the steak into one inch (2.5 cm) pieces and roughly chop the carrots and onions. Put the meat with the vegetables and soup in an ovenproof casserole. Put the flour in a small bowl and gradually stir in the water and mix to a smooth paste, add the stock cube, seasoning and herbs and stir into the casserole.

Cover and cook at 325°F, 160°C, Gas No. 3 for about 3½ hours or until tender. The time will vary with the cut of stewing steak used.

Taste and check seasoning. This is delicious served with potatoes and a green vegetable. Serves 4.

1 lb stewing steak
3 carrots, peeled
3 onions, peeled
1 small can tomato soup
the small can when emptied
    filled with cold water
1 oz flour
1 beef stock cube
salt and pepper
pinch mixed dried herbs

450 gm stewing steak
3 carrots, peeled
3 onions, peeled
1 small can tomato soup
the small can when emptied
    filled with cold water
25 gm flour
1 beef stock cube
salt and pepper
pinch mixed dried herbs

1 lb good raw minced beef
6 oz potatoes, finely diced
4 oz carrots, finely diced
1 large onion, finely
    chopped
1½ level teaspoons salt
plenty of pepper
Pastry:
12 oz plain flour
3 oz hard margarine
3 oz lard
about 4 tablespoons cold
    water to mix
milk or beaten egg to glaze

450 gm good raw minced
    beef
175 gm potatoes, finely
    diced
100 gm carrots, finely diced
1 large onion, finely
    chopped
1½ level teaspoons salt
plenty of pepper

Pastry:

350 gm plain flour
75 gm hard margarine
75 gm lard
about 4 tablespoons cold
*   water to mix*
milk or beaten egg to glaze

Place the beef, potato, carrot, onion, salt and pepper in a bowl and mix thoroughly.

Sieve the flour into a bowl and rub in the fats until the mixture resembles fine breadcrumbs.

Add sufficient water to mix to a firm dough. Roll out $\frac{2}{3}$ of the pastry on a floured table to an oblong and use to line a deep Swiss roll tin approximately 11 × 7 × 1$\frac{1}{2}$ inches (27.5 × 17.5 × 3.75 cm).

Lay the meat mixture in the pastry and press down evenly. Roll out the remaining pastry to form an oblong for the lid. Damp the edges of the pie, position lid and press edges well together. Trim off the surplus pastry,

crimp the edge and decorate the top with the pastry trimmings.

Brush the top with milk or beaten egg to glaze and make two small slits in the centre of the pie. Bake in the oven at 425°F, 220°C, Gas No. 7 for 20-25 minutes until lightly browned, then reduce the temperature to 350°F, 180°C, Gas No. 4 and continue cooking for a further 35-40 minutes. Serve hot. Serves 6.

Slow roast brisket

A good lean piece of brisket slow roasts beautifully. Don't expect the middle to be pink but do expect it to be tender. It makes an economical Sunday roast.

Ask your butcher to prepare the brisket for you by removing all the excess fat and bone. Put the meat in a small meat tin, add the stock cube and sufficient water to give a depth of 1 inch (2.5 cm). Season with salt and pepper. Cover the tin with a lid or piece of foil. Put in a hot oven at 425°F, 220°C, Gas No. 7 for 30 minutes. Then lower the heat to 300°F, 150°C, Gas No. 2 for 50 minutes to the lb (450 gm) of meat. Turn the heat up to 400°F, 200°C, Gas No. 6 for the last 45 minutes of the cooking time to allow roast potatoes to brown and a Yorkshire pudding to cook.

Make a gravy from the stock and meat juices. Serve with Yorkshire pudding and roast potatoes.

Serves 6.

3 lb lean brisket, boned and rolled
1 beef stock cube
$\frac{1}{2}$-$\frac{3}{4}$ pint water
salt and pepper

1. 3 kg lean brisket, boned and rolled
1 beef stock cube
300—450 ml water
salt and pepper

Carbonnade of beef

$1\frac{1}{2}$ lb chuck steak
$1\frac{1}{2}$ oz dripping
$\frac{1}{2}$ lb onions, sliced
2 large carrots, sliced
$1\frac{1}{2}$ oz flour
$\frac{1}{2}$ pint pale ale
$\frac{1}{4}$ pint beef stock
1 rounded tablespoon brown sugar
$1\frac{1}{2}$ teaspoons brown mustard
$1\frac{1}{2}$ level teaspoons salt
pepper
1 bayleaf
675 gm chuck steak
40 gm dripping
225 gm onions, sliced
2 large carrots, sliced
40 gm flour
300 ml pale ale
150 ml beef stock
1 rounded tablespoon brown sugar
$1\frac{1}{2}$ teaspoons brown mustard
$1\frac{1}{2}$ level teaspoons salt
pepper
1 bayleaf

Cut the meat into $\frac{1}{2}$ inch (1.25 cm) thick strips.

Melt the dripping in a pan and quickly brown the meat, lift out with a slotted spoon and put on one side. Add the onions and carrots to the dripping remaining in the pan and fry until golden brown. Stir in the flour and cook for a minute, then gradually blend in the pale ale and stock. Bring to the boil stirring until thickened. Add the sugar, mustard, seasoning and bayleaf and return the meat to the pan. Cover and simmer gently for 2 hours or until the meat is tender.

Taste and check seasoning and remove the bayleaf.

Serves 4-6.

Cook's Tip

Once cider or beer is opened and used for cooking, any that is left should be decanted into a small bottle to be kept in the refrigerator and used within a month.

Cottage pie

a little dripping
1 lb good raw mince
1 large onion, chopped
2 carrots, peeled and diced
$\frac{1}{4}$ level teaspoon mixed dried herbs
2 level tablespoons tomato puree
1 oz flour
$\frac{1}{2}$ pint beef stock
1 level teaspoon salt
black pepper
a little gravy browning
1$\frac{1}{2}$ lb potatoes
1 oz butter
a little milk

a little dripping
450 gm good raw mince
1 large onion, chopped
2 carrots, peeled and diced
$\frac{1}{4}$ level teaspoon mixed dried herbs
2 level tablespoons tomato puree
25 gm flour
300 ml beef stock
1 level teaspoon salt
black pepper
a little gravy browning
675 gm potatoes
25 gm butter
a little milk

Melt the dripping in a pan, add the mince, onion and carrots and fry stirring frequently to brown. Stir in the herbs, tomato puree and flour and cook for a minute. Add the stock and seasoning and bring to the boil, stirring until thickened and then add a little gravy browning if liked. Cover the pan and simmer for about 45 minutes or until the meat and vegetables are tender. Turn into a 2$\frac{1}{2}$ pint (1.4 l) oven-proof pie dish and leave to cool.

Meanwhile cook the potatoes in boiling salted water until tender. Drain well, mash with the butter and milk and season to taste.

Using a fork, cover the top of the meat with the potato, spreading evenly.

When required bake in the oven at 375°F, 190°C, Gas No. 5 for 30-40 minutes or until the pie is hot through. Serves 4.

Scottish pressed beef

2½-3 lb salted brisket of beef, boned
1 large onion, roughly chopped
8 cloves
3 bayleaves
2 carrots, sliced
2 sticks celery, sliced
8 peppercorns

1. 1–1. 3 kg salted brisket of beef, boned
1 large onion, roughly chopped
8 cloves
3 bayleaves
2 carrots, sliced
2 sticks celery, sliced
8 peppercorns

Place the brisket in a saucepan just large enough to take it. Add sufficient water just to cover the joint, and add all the remaining ingredients. Bring to the boil very slowly and lift off any scum with a slotted spoon. Cover the pan and simmer very gently for 3-3½ hours until the meat is very tender. It may be necessary to add a little more boiling water to the pan during cooking time.

Lift out the meat carefully from the saucepan and remove any cloves or peppercorns that may be attached to it. Place in a cake tin which is just a little too small for it and cover with a saucer or plate and then several weights or heavy tins. Leave to become quite cold and then chill in the refrigerator for several hours, preferably overnight.

To serve, turn the meat out carefully, cut downwards into thin slices and serve with a selection of salads. Serves 6.

Crunchy pork and cabbage

This dish can be prepared in advance as far as simmering until tender with all ingredients added except peas and cabbage; then cool quickly. Just before serving cook peas and cabbage and continue as below.

$1\frac{1}{4}$-$1\frac{1}{2}$ lb lean belly of pork
2 oz butter
2 large onions, sliced
2 cloves garlic, crushed
$\frac{1}{2}$ lb carrots, diced
2 level teaspoons curry
    powder
1 tablespoon soy sauce
$\frac{3}{4}$ level teaspoon salt
pepper to taste
3 tablespoons water
8 oz white cabbage,
    shredded
8 oz frozen peas

550–675 gm lean belly of
    pork
50 gm butter
2 large onions, sliced
2 cloves garlic, crushed
225 gm carrots, diced
2 level teaspoons curry
    powder
1 tablespoon soy sauce
$\frac{3}{4}$ level teaspoon salt
pepper to taste
3 tablespoons water
225 gm white cabbage,
    shredded
225 gm frozen peas

Remove the skin from the pork and cut away any bones and gristle, then cut into neat cubes.

Heat the butter in a pan and add the pork, fry gently for 5 minutes, stirring frequently. Add onions, garlic and carrots and continue cooking for a further 10-15 minutes, stirring occasionally to prevent sticking. Stir in the curry powder, soy sauce, salt, pepper and water and cover the pan. Simmer gently for 15-20 minutes or until the pork is tender.

Meanwhile cook cabbage and peas for 3-5 minutes in boiling salted water until the cabbage is still very crisp but just tender and drain thoroughly. Stir the cabbage and peas into the meat mixture, taste and check seasoning and serve at once. Serves 4.

Spicy pork balls

It is very economical to buy pork knuckles or hocks but it does take time to get the meat off the bone. So if you are very busy buy 12 oz (350 gm) boneless spare rib pork.

Remove the skin from the pork and then strip the flesh from the bones and discard any excess fat and gristle. Put through a fine mincer with one onion and the bread. Combine this mixture with salt and pepper and bind with the egg. Divide into 12 and shape into even sized balls with lightly floured hands so that the mixture is not sticky.

Heat the oil in a pan and fry the meat balls until browned all over. Lift out with a slotted spoon and put on one side. Finely slice the remaining onion, add to the pan and fry for a few minutes, then drain off any fat remaining in the pan.

Mix together the remaining ingredients, add to the pan, and bring to the boil, stirring. Return the meat balls to the pan, cover and simmer for about 30 minutes or until tender. Remove the lid and boil rapidly for 2 to 3 minutes to let the sauce thicken slightly, or if liked the sauce may be thickened with a little cornflour.

Serve with plain boiled noodles or rice. Serves 4.

2 pork knuckles or hocks
2 onions, peeled
2 oz white bread
1 level teaspoon salt
pepper
1 egg, beaten
a little flour
2 tablespoons oil
4 level tablespoons brown sugar
1 level teaspoon paprika pepper
1 level tablespoon tomato puree
1 level teaspoon salt
1 tablespoon Worcestershire sauce
½ pint water
2 tablespoons vinegar

2 pork knuckles or hocks
2 onions, peeled
50 gm white bread
1 level teaspoon salt
pepper
1 egg, beaten
a little flour
2 tablespoons oil
4 level tablespoons brown sugar
1 level teaspoon paprika pepper
1 level tablespoon tomato puree
1 level teaspoon salt
1 tablespoon Worcestershire sauce
300 ml water
2 tablespoons vinegar

Steak and kidney pie

The pastry is my mother's recipe. It is essential to use a hard margarine straight from the fridge. I use this same pastry for fruit pies too.

1 lb skirt beef
4 oz ox kidney
1 oz flour
1 oz dripping
1 large onion, chopped
$\frac{1}{2}$ pint beef stock
1 teaspoon salt
ground black pepper
4 oz mushrooms, sliced

Quick family flaky pastry:

8 oz strong plain flour
$\frac{1}{2}$ teaspoon salt
6 oz hard margarine
about 9 tablespoons or a
    scant $\frac{1}{4}$ pint cold water
a little beaten egg to glaze

450 gm skirt beef
100 gm ox kidney
25 gm flour
25 gm dripping
1 large onion, chopped
300 ml beef stock
1 teaspoon salt
ground black pepper
100 gm mushrooms, sliced

Quick family flaky pastry:

225 gm strong plain flour
$\frac{1}{2}$ teaspoon salt
175 gm hard margarine
about 9 tablespoons or a
    scant 150 ml cold water
a little beaten egg to glaze

Cut the steak and kidney into 1 inch (2.5 cm) pieces, put in a polythene bag with the flour and toss until well coated. Melt the dripping in a saucepan, add the meat and fry with the onion until browned. Stir in the stock and seasoning and bring to the boil. Partially cover the pan and simmer for about 1$\frac{1}{2}$ hours, then stir in the mushrooms and continue cooking for a further 30 minutes or until the meat is tender. Taste and check seasoning, turn into a 1$\frac{1}{2}$ pint (900 ml) pie dish and allow to become cold. Put a pie funnel or handleless cup in the centre.

For the pastry: sift the flour and salt into a mixing bowl. Coarsely grate the margarine into the bowl. Stir in just sufficient water to make a firm dough and then roll out on a lightly floured surface to make a strip about $\frac{1}{2}$ inch (1.25 cm) thick and 6 inches (15 cm) wide. Fold the pastry in three and give it a quarter turn to the left. Roll out again into a strip and fold in three. Wrap the pastry in foil and chill in the fridge for 30 minutes.

Heat the oven to 425°F, 220°C, Gas No. 7.

Roll out the pastry on a lightly floured table and use to cover the pie, seal and crimp the edges and use any pastry trimming to decorate the top with pastry leaves. If there is any leftover pastry this may be used to make a pasty or turnover.

Brush the pie with a little beaten egg and make a small hole in the centre for the steam to escape. Bake in the oven for 40 minutes and if the pastry is browning too much reduce the heat to 350°F, 180°C, Gas No. 4 for a further 15 minutes to cook the pastry until it is golden brown and the meat is hot through. Serves 4 to 6.

Shoulder of lamb with green stuffing

New Zealand lamb is ideal cooked in this way. If spinach is unobtainable use masses of chopped parsley mixed with a little thyme. There will be lots of juices in the meat tin for gravy.

3½ lb shoulder of lamb, boned
salt and pepper
Stuffing:
8 oz packet frozen chopped spinach, thawed
4 oz lamb's liver
1 oz butter
1 large onion, chopped
1 clove garlic, crushed
2 oz fresh brown bread crumbs
seasoning

1. 5 kg shoulder of lamb, boned
salt and pepper
Stuffing:
225 gm packet frozen chopped spinach, thawed
100 gm lamb's liver
25 gm butter
1 large onion, chopped
1 clove garlic, crushed
50 gm fresh brown bread crumbs
seasoning

Heat the oven to 350°F, 180°C, Gas No. 4. Open the shoulder out flat and season well.

Cook spinach as directed and drain. Chop the liver into small pieces and then melt the butter in a pan and fry the liver with the onion and garlic for about 3 minutes. Stir in the spinach and breadcrumbs and season very well. Put the stuffing into the cavity in the meat and secure with skewers. Place the meat in a roasting tin and roast in the oven for 1¾-2½ hours or until the meat is tender. Make the gravy from the juices in the pan. Serves 6 to 8.

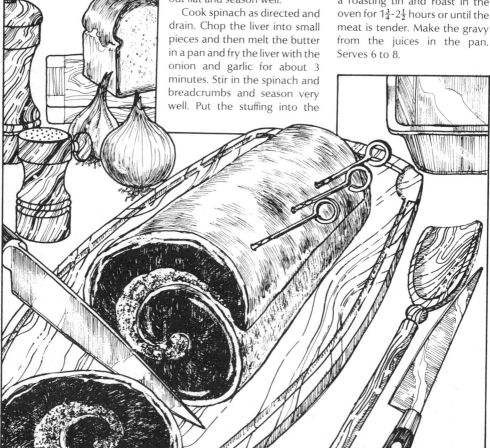

Chicken and duck

1½ oz butter
2 tablespoons oil
4 chicken joints
1 large onion, chopped
½ can concentrated orange
   juice, thawed
1 chicken stock cube
¼ pint water
4 sprigs of fresh tarragon,
   chopped
½ oz cornflour
2 tablespoons water
5 oz carton soured cream

40 gm butter
2 tablespoons oil
4 chicken joints
1 large onion, chopped
½ can concentrated orange
   juice, thawed
1 chicken stock cube
150 ml water
4 sprigs of fresh tarragon,
   chopped
12.5 gm cornflour
2 tablespoons water
150 ml carton soured cream

Chicken with orange tarragon sauce

Melt the butter and heat the oil in a large frying pan and brown the chicken on all sides. Lift out with a slotted spoon and put on one side. If liked the skin may be removed.

Add the onion to the pan and cook for 2-3 minutes. Stir in the orange juice, stock cube and water. Return the chicken joints to the pan and add the tarragon. Cover the pan and simmer for about 30 minutes or until the chicken is tender, basting and turning occasionally.

Lift out the chicken and place on a warm serving dish. Blend the cornflour with the water and stir into the sauce, then bring to the boil, stirring until thickened.

Taste and check seasoning, cool slightly and then stir in the soured cream and spoon over the chicken. Garnish with fresh sprigs of tarragon. Serves 4.

Frozen concentrated orange juice is excellent for cooking and inexpensive when you think that each 6 fl oz (178 ml) can contains the concentrated juice of 11 oranges.

I find dried tarragon lacking in flavour, so if this is the only thing to hand, I often use fresh chopped chives instead, and the flavour is nearly as good.

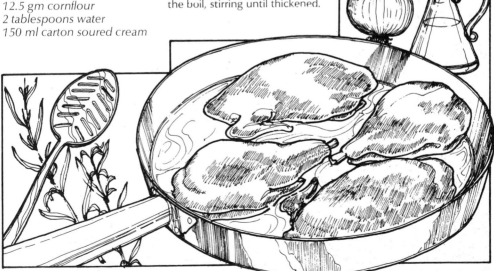

3 lb cooked chicken
1 small fresh pineapple
juice of 1 lemon
½ pint thick home-made
    mayonnaise (see p.60)
salt
freshly ground black pepper
1 oz walnuts, chopped
lettuce hearts and
    watercress to garnish

1. 3 kg cooked chicken
1 small fresh pineapple
juice of 1 lemon
300 ml thick home-made
    mayonnaise (see p. 60)
salt
freshly ground black pepper
25 gm walnuts, chopped
lettuce hearts and watercress
    to garnish

Summer chicken in lemon mayonnaise

This is a very good way of using up turkey after Christmas and makes a delicious special cold supper dish when you have friends in. Canned pineapple may be used if liked but the flavour is rather sweeter than using fresh pineapple. If preparing ahead mix the lemon mayonnaise with the two different coloured meats and put in plastic containers. Prepare the pineapple and then assemble 30 minutes before the meal.

Remove the meat from the chicken. Slice the white meat and cut the dark meat into bite-sized pieces.

Slice the pineapple and remove the skin and centre core. Cut 3 slices in half and reserve for garnish, and chop the remainder. Stir the lemon juice into the mayonnaise (p.60) and season to taste. Mix 3-4 tablespoons (45-60 ml) mayonnaise with the dark meat and arrange it on a serving dish. Cover with the chopped pineapple and arrange the slices of white meat on top and then coat with the remaining mayonnaise.

Sprinkle over the chopped walnuts and garnish the dish with lettuce hearts, watercress and the halved slices of pineapple. Serves 6.

Spanish chicken

4 chicken quarters
2 tablespoons oil
3 Spanish onions, sliced
1 clove garlic, crushed
$\frac{1}{4}$ pint chicken stock
1 teaspoon mixed dried herbs
salt and pepper
1 lb ripe tomatoes, peeled and sliced
16 stuffed green olives
1 tablespoon cornflour
1 tablespoon water

4 chicken quarters
2 tablespoons oil
3 Spanish onions, sliced
1 clove garlic, crushed
150 ml chicken stock
1 teaspoon mixed dried herbs
salt and pepper
450 gm ripe tomatoes, peeled and sliced
16 stuffed green olives
1 tablespoon cornflour
1 tablespoon water

Fry the chicken quarters in oil until they are golden brown on both sides. Remove from the pan and set on one side. Add the onions and garlic to the pan and fry for 3 minutes.

Skin the chicken quarters if liked and then return to the pan with the stock, herbs, seasoning and sliced tomatoes. Cover the pan and simmer for 30 minutes or until the chicken is quite tender when pierced with the point of a sharp knife.

Lift out the chicken and place on a warm serving dish. Add the olives to the pan, blend the cornflour with the water and a tablespoon of the hot sauce and stir into the pan. Bring to the boil, stirring until thickened and then simmer for 3 minutes. Taste and check seasoning and then spoon over the chicken joints. Serves 4.

Chicken in lemon sauce

This recipe is perfectly suited to a real old-fashioned boiling fowl. Though you may have difficulty in getting one, they should be cheaper per pound than a roasting bird. Boiling fowls have a really good flavour, but no definite cooking time can be given as it depends on the age of the bird.

4 lb boiling fowl with giblets
thinly pared rind of 2 lemons
2 sprigs parsley
2 onions, quartered
1 carrot, quartered
bouquet garni
salt and pepper
Sauce:
2 oz butter
2 oz flour
$\frac{1}{2}$ pint milk
juice of 2 lemons
chopped fresh parsley

1.8 kg boiling fowl with
giblets
thinly pared rind of 2 lemons
2 sprigs parsley
2 onions, quartered
1 carrot, quartered
bouquet garni
salt and pepper
Sauce:
50 gm butter
50 gm flour
300 ml milk
juice of 2 lemons
chopped fresh parsley

Rinse the fowl with cold water. Put giblets, the rind of half a lemon and a sprig of parsley inside the bird. Secure the legs with a skewer or string. Put the bird in a saucepan with the rest of the lemon rind, second parsley sprig, onions, carrot, bouquet garni and seasoning. Pour in enough water to cover and bring to the boil and simmer for 2 to 4 hours or until bird is tender. To test, remove the string or skewer and raise drumstick to see if leg joint is loose.

Remove the bird from the saucepan and discard giblets, lemon rind and parsley inside. Set on a serving dish and keep hot while you make the sauce.

Skim the fat off stock in the saucepan and strain off $\frac{1}{2}$ pint (300 ml) stock. Set aside and use the remainder for soup.

In another saucepan melt butter, stir in the flour and cook for 2 minutes, stirring. Remove the pan from the heat and gradually add the milk, stirring constantly, then add the reserved stock. Return pan to the heat and bring sauce to the boil, still stirring. Simmer until the sauce has thickened, then stir in the lemon juice. Taste and check seasoning, pour the sauce over the chicken, sprinkle with parsley and serve. Serves 6 to 8.

English roast duckling

4½-5 lb duckling
salt

2–2.3 kg duckling
salt

To carve the duck, use sharp kitchen scissors and cut the duck's breast in half starting from the neck end. Cut along the length of the breast bone. Then cut through the backbone to split the bird in half. If you like cut along the backbone as well, remove the backbone and put it in the stockpot so that you serve less bone on the plate. Cut each half of the bird into 2, making a slanting cut between the ribs to separate the wing and the leg. You will now have 4 good portions.

Preheat the oven to 400°F, 200°C, Gas No. 6. For the stock, take the giblets and put them in a casserole with a little onion, ground pepper, stock cube and ¾ pint (450 ml) water. Cover and put in the oven on the lower shelf.

Prick the duck all over with a sharp-pronged fork. Rub with salt and put on a rack or trivet in a roasting tin. Roast, without basting for about 1½ hours. Test to see if the duck is done by piercing the thickest part of the leg with a skewer. If the juices run clear, the bird is ready. Put in the stuffing (see below) to cook with the duck for the last half hour of cooking time. Rest the duck for 5 minutes before carving.

Make a gravy from 2 tablespoons duck fat heated in a pan mixed with 1 level tablespoon flour Stir in the strained giblet stock from the casserole and tip the juices from the inside of the bird into the gravy making sure that you add no extra fat. Add a little gravy browning if liked and check seasoning. Serve the duck with sage and onion stuffing and apple sauce.

Sage and onion stuffing

2 onions
1 oz butter
4 oz fresh white bread
   crumbs
1 teaspoon dried sage
½ teaspoon salt
ground black pepper

2 onions
25 gm butter
100 gm fresh white bread
   crumbs
1 teaspoon dried sage
½ teaspoon salt
ground black pepper

Butter well an 8 inch (20 cm) shallow ovenproof dish. Peel the onions. (Add any onion skins and odd pieces of onion to the giblet stock.) Chop the onions roughly and put in a pan. Cover with water and bring to the boil. Simmer until barely tender for about 5 minutes. Drain really well, pressing out all excess liquid. Return the onions to the pan and add butter. Stir to melt the butter, then add bread crumbs, sage, salt and plenty of black pepper. Spread over the dish and dot with more butter. Bake with the duck for about 30 minutes until pale brown and crispy.

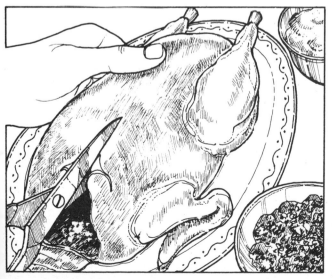

Glazed roast duckling with orange sauce

4½-5 lb duckling

Glaze:
1 tablespoon redcurrant jelly
1 teaspoon Soy sauce

Sauce:
2 oranges
2 tablespoons duck fat
½ oz flour
about ½ pint giblet stock (see below)
2 tablespoons port or Madeira
1 tablespoon redcurrant jelly
salt
ground black pepper

2–2,3 kg duckling

Glaze:
1 tablespoon redcurrant jelly
1 teaspoon Soy sauce

Sauce:
2 oranges
2 tablespoons duck fat
12.5 gm flour
about 300 ml giblet stock (see below)
2 tablespoons port or Madeira (optional)
1 tablespoon redcurrant jelly
salt
ground black pepper

Cook's Tip

The glaze is delicious but don't expect it to be as crisp as if you had just open-roasted the bird. You can also roast it as below without the glaze but with the orange sauce.

To reheat the carved duckling, put the joints well spaced out on an uncovered roasting tin and reheat in a preheated oven at 425° F, 220° C, Gas No. 7 for about 10-15 minutes.

Preheat the oven to 400°F, 200°C, Gas No.6.

For the stock: take the giblets and put them in a casserole with a little onion, ground black pepper, stock cube and ¾ pint (450 ml) water. Cover and put in the oven on the lower shelf.

Prick the duck all over with a sharp-pronged fork. Rub with plenty of salt and put on a rack or trivet in a roasting tin. Roast without basting for 1¼ hours.

Take the duck out, tip any juices from the inside of it into a measuring jug and put the bird on a board. Mix the redcurrant jelly and Soy sauce together and spread over the top of the duck. Skim off all the fat from the roasting tin and add remaining meat juices to those in the measuring jug. Put the fat aside. Return the bird to the oven for about 15 minutes until the skin is crisp and browned. Test to see if it is done by piercing the thickest part of the leg with a skewer. If the juices run clear and slightly yellow in colour, the duck is done. Save any more juices from the roasting tin to add to the sauce and keep the duck hot.

Meanwhile prepare the sauce: carefully peel 1 orange, removing the zest only. Chop finely and simmer in a little water for 3 minutes then drain. This is to add to the sauce later. Squeeze the juice out of 1½ of the oranges and finely slice the remaining half for garnish.

Measure 2 tablespoons duck fat into a small pan and add the flour. Cook for a few minutes, allowing to colour a pale brown.

Make the duck juices up to ½ pint (300 ml) with stock, add to the pan and stir until thickened. Add port or Madeira if liked, redcurrant jelly and orange juice. Season with salt and ground black pepper. Add a little gravy browning, if you wish.

Lift the duck onto a serving dish and decorate with water-cress and orange slices. Serve with the sauce, an orange salad, peas and creamed or new potatoes.

Supper dishes

Omelettes

To make the classic French omelette you must first get the pan very hot before adding the butter. Work quickly when the mixture goes into the pan, and serve when the centre of the omelette is hardly set.

2 eggs
1 tablespoon water
salt and pepper
½oz butter
chopped parsley

*2 eggs
1 tablespoon water
salt and pepper
12.5 gm butter
chopped parsley*

Place eggs, water and seasoning in a bowl and beat lightly with a fork. Heat the omelette pan until hot, add the butter and when hot and frothy pour in the egg mixture. Using the fork, quickly draw mixture from sides of the pan to the centre to allow the uncooked egg to run underneath, shake pan and leave for a few seconds.

Draw the pan from the heat, loosen the sides, fold the omelette in three, tap the pan and slip onto a warm plate. Sprinkle with a little chopped parsley and serve at once.
Serves 1

Fillings:
Fine herbs: 1 tablespoon chopped fresh herbs added to the egg mixture.
Cheese: 1 oz (25 gm) grated cheese sprinkled on the omelette before folding.
Ham: 1 oz (25 gm) diced cooked ham, sprinkled on the omelette before folding.
Tomato: 1 tomato, peeled, seeded and finely chopped and cooked in a little butter. Season well and spoon onto the omelette before folding.

Mushroom: Quarter 1-2 oz (25-50 gm) small mushrooms and cook in a little butter for 5 minutes, season well and spoon onto the omelette before folding.
Spanish: Peel and finely dice a small onion, seed and finely shred half a small green pepper and then cook in a little butter or oil for 5 minutes. Stir in a peeled and sliced tomato. Stir into the egg mixture and make as usual, but do not fold, slip flat onto a plate.

Baked onions

4 large onions or 8 medium
   sized onions, peeled
a knob of dripping
1 lb raw minced beef
2 large tomatoes, peeled
   and chopped
1 level teaspoon dried
   thyme
1 level teaspoon salt
pepper
$\frac{1}{2}$ teaspoon Worcestershire
   sauce
1 level teaspoon paprika
   pepper
$1\frac{1}{2}$ oz butter
3 level tablespoons flour
$\frac{1}{2}$ pint milk

*4 large onions or 8 medium
   sized onions, peeled
a knob of dripping
450 gm raw minced beef
2 large tomatoes, peeled and
   chopped
1 level teaspoon dried thyme
1 level teaspoon salt
pepper
$\frac{1}{2}$ teaspoon Worcestershire
   sauce
1 level teaspoon paprika
   pepper
40 gm butter
3 level tablespoons flour
300 ml milk*

Place the onions in a saucepan, barely cover with water and bring to the boil. Cover the pan and simmer for 25 minutes. Then drain the onions and reserve $\frac{1}{4}$ pint (150 ml) of the liquor. Remove the centres of the onions.

Melt the dripping and fry the mince gently for 5-10 minutes, stirring frequently. Add the tomatoes, thyme, salt and pepper, Worcestershire sauce and paprika and cook for a further 3 to 4 minutes. Spoon the meat mixture carefully into the onion cavities.

Spoon the remaining meat mixture into the base of a 4 pint (2.3 l) casserole or a foil-lined baking tin. Stand the onions on top. Cover the casserole or close the foil and cook in the oven at 350°F, 180°C, Gas No. 4 for 1-1$\frac{1}{2}$ hours or until the onions are tender.

Meanwhile melt the butter in a pan, chop the onion centres and fry gently for 10 minutes without colouring. Stir in the flour and cook for a minute, then gradually add the onion liquor and milk and bring to the boil, stirring frequently. Season well and simmer for 3 minutes.

Serve the onions on a spoonful of meat mixture with the sauce handed separately. Delicious served with hot crusty bread. Serves 4.

Rösti

2 lb large potatoes
½ teaspoon salt
4 tablespoons salad oil
1 oz butter

900 gm large potatoes
½ teaspoon salt
4 tablespoons salad oil
25 gm butter

Scrub potatoes and boil in salted water for 10-15 minutes or until the point of a knife can be inserted into the potato for about an inch (2.5 cm) before meeting resistance. Drain the potatoes and when cool, peel.

Leave the potatoes to become quite cold, then grate coarsely and sprinkle with salt. Melt half the oil and butter in a non-stick pan. Add the potato and flatten with a fish slice. Fry over a low heat for about 30 minutes.

Using the fish slice, lift the sides of the potato up to check that it is golden brown and then turn out onto a large plate. Put the remainder of the oil and butter into the pan and heat. Slide potato cake off the plate into the hot fat and brown the second side. Serve at once.

Fried onions and bacon are often served in the Rösti. They should be sandwiched in the potato as it is put in the frying pan. Serves 4.

Supper baked eggs

6 rashers back bacon
6 tomatoes
12 mushrooms
butter
6 eggs

6 rashers back bacon
6 tomatoes
12 mushrooms
butter
6 eggs

Remove the rind and any bone from the bacon and cut each rasher in half. Halve the tomatoes. Place two pieces of bacon and two tomato halves and mushrooms in six small ovenproof dishes. Dot each mushroom with a knob of butter and bake in the centre of the oven heated to 400°F, 200°C, Gas No.6 for about 10 minutes.

Crack an egg into the centre of each dish and bake for a further 5 minutes.

Serve at once with garlic rolls (p.54). Serves 6.

Mols spaghetti

Cook the spaghetti in plenty of boiling salted water for 12 minutes or until just tender, then drain very well.

Meanwhile cut the rind from the bacon and cut into strips. Melt the butter in a pan and fry the bacon until it is pale golden brown. Slice the mushrooms and add to the pan and cook for 2 minutes, then blend the bacon and mushroom mixture into the cooked spaghetti.

Stir in the egg, salt and pepper to taste. Cook over a low heat, stirring with a fork until the egg has scrambled. Pile onto a serving dish and if liked sprinkle the top with a little parsley. Serves 1.

3 oz spaghetti
2 oz bacon
½ oz butter
2 oz button mushrooms
1 egg, beaten
salt and pepper

75 gm spaghetti
50 gm bacon
12.5 gm butter
50 gm button mushrooms
1 egg, beaten
salt and pepper

Cook's Tip

A quick and easy supper dish for when you are on your own.

Puddings

Home-made yogurt

1 pint milk
2 heaped teaspoons bought
  yogurt (the culture)
1 heaped tablespoon dried
  milk powder

600 ml milk
2 heaped teaspoons bought
  yogurt (the culture)
1 heaped tablespoon dried
  milk powder

Heat the milk to boiling, then cool in a bowl of cold water to about 112°F, 60°C, hot bath temperature. Put yogurt in a bowl with the milk and then whisk in the dried milk.

Cover and put either in a linen cupboard for 12 hours or in a wide-mouthed vacuum flask for 6 hours. Or use a yogurt-making kit.

Caramel custard

Caramel:
3 oz granulated sugar
3 tablespoons water
Custard:
4 eggs
1½ oz caster sugar
a few drops of vanilla
  essence
1 pint milk

Caramel:
75 gm granulated sugar
3 tablespoons water
Custard:
4 eggs
40 gm caster sugar
a few drops of vanilla essence
600 ml milk

To make caramel: put the sugar and water in a heavy saucepan and dissolve the sugar over a low heat. Bring to the boil and boil until the syrup is pale golden brown. Remove from the heat and quickly pour into the bottom of a 1½ pint (900 ml) charlotte mould or souffée dish.

For the custard: mix together eggs, sugar and vanilla essence. Warm the milk in a saucepan over a low heat until it is hand-hot, then pour it onto the egg mixture, stirring constantly.

Butter the sides of the mould or dish above the caramel. Strain the custard into it and place in a roasting tin half filled with hot water. Bake in an oven preheated to 300°F, 150°C, Gas No. 2 for 1½ hours or until a knife inserted in the centre comes out clean.

Do not worry if the custard takes longer to cook than the time given; it will set eventually. Don't increase the oven temperature or the custard will have bubbles in it.

Remove the custard from the oven and leave to cool completely for at least 12 hours or overnight in the refrigerator. Turn out carefully onto a flat serving dish. Serves 4.

Cinnamon apple pancakes

Sift the flour and salt into a bowl and make a well in the centre. Add egg and gradually stir in half the milk. Using a whisk blend in the flour from the sides of the bowl, beat well until mixture is smooth and stir in the remaining milk and oil.

Heat a little oil in an 8 inch (20 cm) frying pan. When it is hot pour off any excess oil and spoon about 2 tablespoons (30 ml) of batter into the pan. Tip and rotate the pan so that the batter spreads out and thinly covers the base. Cook for about a minute until pale brown underneath, then turn over with a palette knife and cook for another minute. Slip pancake out of the pan and make about 7 more pancakes with the remaining batter.

For the filling: in a saucepan, gently cook the apples, cinnamon, sugar and 4 oz (100 gm) butter for about 20 minutes or until the apples are tender, stirring occasionally.

Spread the pancakes flat, spoon some of the filling on to each and roll them up. In a large frying pan heat the remaining butter with a little oil and fry the pancakes on all sides until golden brown.

Pile on a warm serving dish, sprinkle with sugar and cinnamon and serve with cream or ice cream. Serves 4.

Batter:
4 oz flour
$\frac{1}{4}$ teaspoon salt
1 egg
$\frac{1}{2}$ pint milk
1 tablespoon salad oil
oil for frying
Filling:
4 large Bramley apples,
    peeled, cored and sliced
$\frac{1}{4}$ teaspoon ground
    cinnamon
6 oz demerara sugar
5 oz butter

Batter:
100 gm flour
$\frac{1}{4}$ teaspoon salt
1 egg
300 ml milk
1 tablespoon salad oil
oil for frying
Filling:
4 large Bramley apples,
    peeled, cored and sliced
$\frac{1}{4}$ teaspoon ground
    cinnamon
175 gm demerara sugar
150 gm butter

Lemon meringue pie

One of the English classics. Not a simple pudding to make, so the instructions should be followed exactly for success. Ideally make and bake on the same day.

First make the pastry: put the flour in a bowl, add the fats cut in small pieces and rub in with the fingertips until the mixture resembles fine bread crumbs. Mix the egg yolk, sugar and water together, stir into the dry ingredients and bind them together. Roll out the pastry on a floured board, line a 9 inch (22.5 cm) flan tin and chill for 30 minutes.

Heat the oven to 425°F, 220°C, Gas No. 7 with a thick baking sheet in it. Line the flan with greaseproof paper, weigh down with baking beans and bake blind for 15 minutes.

Meanwhile prepare the filling: Finely grate the rind and

6 oz plain flour
2 oz butter
2 oz lard
1 egg yolk
½ oz caster sugar
2 teaspoons cold water

Filling:
2 large lemons
1½ oz cornflour
½ pint water
2 egg yolks
3 oz caster sugar
Meringue topping:
3 egg whites
4½ oz caster sugar

175 gm plain flour
50 gm butter
50 gm lard
1 egg yolk
12.5 gm caster sugar
2 teaspoons cold water

Filling:
2 large lemons
40 gm cornflour
300 ml water
2 eggs yolks
75 gm caster sugar
Meringue topping:
3 eggs whites
125 gm caster sugar

squeeze the juice from the lemons and put in a bowl with the cornflour. Add 2 table-spoons of water and blend to form a smooth paste. Boil the remaining water and pour it onto the cornflour mixture. Return to the pan, bring to the boil and simmer for 3 minutes until thick, stirring continuously. Remove from the heat and add the egg yolks blended with the sugar. Return to the heat for a moment to thicken the sauce and then cool slightly.

Remove the beans and greaseproof paper from the flan

and spoon in the filling.

For the topping: whisk the egg whites with an electric or rotary whisk until they form stiff peaks and add the sugar a teaspoonful at a time, whisking well after each addition. Spoon the meringue over the lemon filling being careful to spread it right up to the edge of the pastry and leaving no air spaces. Return to the oven and reduce the heat to 325°F, 160°C, Gas No. 3 for about 30 minutes or until a pale golden brown.

Serve the pie either warm or cold. Serves 6.

Helen's chocolate layer pudding

A deliciously rich pudding, though not a cheap one. It is also a convenient way of using up leftover bread. Make the bread into crumbs in the blender, but if you haven't got one, use 2-3 day old bread and grate it or rub it through a coarse sieve. Serve in a small glass bowl or 4 individual glasses.

4 rounded tablespoons drinking chocolate
1 level tablespoon coffee powder
4 oz fresh white bread crumbs
4 oz demerara sugar
½ pint whipping cream
chocolate flake bar

4 rounded tablespoons drinking chocolate
1 level tablespoon coffee powder
100 gm fresh white bread crumbs
100 gm demerara sugar
300 ml whipping cream
chocolate flake bar

Place the chocolate, coffee powder, breadcrumbs and sugar in a bowl and mix thoroughly. Put the cream in a bowl and whisk with an electric or hand rotary whisk until thick and soft peaks are formed when the whisk is lifted out.

Spread alternate layers of chocolate mixture and cream in a serving dish, starting with the chocolate and finishing with the cream. Leave in a cool place for at least 8-10 hours before serving.

This pudding may be made a day in advance.

Decorate with pieces of chocolate flake before serving. Serves 4.

6-8 large slices of white
  bread
¾ lb rhubarb
½ lb blackcurrants
½ lb granulated sugar
6 tablespoons water
½ lb strawberries
½ lb raspberries

6–8 large slices of white
  bread
350 gm rhubarb
225 gm blackcurrants
225 gm granulated sugar
6 tablespoons water
225 gm strawberries
225 gm raspberries

Summer pudding

The very same fruit filling can be served on its own with fresh cream as a rich red fruit salad. If you find that the suggested fruits are not available substitute others. Loganberries and other currants may be used with either fresh or frozen fruit.

Cut the crusts from the bread and put aside one slice for the top. Use the remainder of the bread to line the base and sides of a 2 pint (a good litre) round, fairly shallow dish.

Cut the rhubarb into ½ inch (1.25 cm) pieces and put with the blackcurrants in a saucepan. Add the sugar and water and bring to the boil. Simmer until barely tender, stirring: this will only take a few minutes. Add the strawberries and raspberries and cook for a further minute.

Turn the mixture into the dish, reserving a little of the juice. Place a slice of bread on top and bend over the top of the sliced bread at the sides towards the centre. Put a saucer on top pressing down a little until the juice rises to the top of the dish. Spoon the juice remaining in the pan down the side of the dish to make sure that every slice is really well soaked and not left white.

Leave to soak until quite cold and then chill overnight in the refrigerator. Turn out just before serving and serve with lots of cream. Serves 4 to 6.

Creme brûlée

This dessert is sheer luxury, and not difficult to make at all. Choose a shallow dish that will withstand being put under the grill. Make the cream custard part a day ahead, then put the sugar topping on 3 hours before serving.

Heat the oven to 325°F, 160°C, Gas No. 3. Butter well a shallow 1½ pint (900 ml) ovenproof dish, or 6-8 small individual dishes. Beat the egg yolks with the sugar. (If you haven't any vanilla sugar but like the flavour, then add a little vanilla essence.) Heat the cream to scalding and gradually beat in the egg yolks.

Pour the mixture into the dish or dishes, stand in a baking tin

4 egg yolks
1 oz caster or vanilla sugar
1 pint single cream
about 2 oz demerara sugar

4 egg yolks
25 gm caster or vanilla sugar
600 ml single cream
about 50 gm demerara sugar

half filled with warm water and bake in the oven for 45 minutes or until set. If using small dishes they will need only 25-30 minutes cooking time. Take out and leave to cool.

Sprinkle the top thickly with demerara sugar and put under a hot grill. Watch carefully until the sugar melts and then caramelizes to a golden brown. Remove and chill before serving for at least 3 hours. This gives time for the hard caramel topping to become less hard and easier to crack and serve. If you leave it considerably longer the caramel will melt and soften, which is not nearly so attractive and doesn't taste so good.

English custard tart

As a variation, add 2 oz (50 gm) mixed dried fruit and some freshly grated lemon rind.

Pastry:
4 oz plain flour
1 oz margarine
1 oz lard
about 4 teaspoons cold
  water to mix

Custard:
2 eggs
1 oz caster sugar
$\frac{1}{2}$ pint milk
a little grated nutmeg

Pastry:
100 gm plain flour
25 gm margarine
25 gm lard
about 4 teaspoons cold
  water to mix

Custard:
2 eggs
25 gm caster sugar
300 ml milk
a little grated nutmeg

Heat the oven to 425°F, 220°C, Gas No. 7 with a baking sheet in it.

Prepare the pastry as usual (see p.12), roll out and line an enamel, tin or foil 7 inch (17.5 cm) flan tin. Fill with baking beans and bake blind for 20 minutes. Remove the beans.

For the custard, beat the eggs and sugar together until blended and then stir in the milk. Pour into the pastry case and sprinkle the top with a little nutmeg. Place in the oven on the hot baking sheet, then reduce the heat to 350°F, 180°C, Gas No. 4 and bake for 40-45 minutes or until the filling is set and a pale golden brown. Serve warm on the day that it is made. Serves 4 to 6.

Syllabub

Quite the easiest of puddings to make, very rich and best served in small individual dishes or glasses. Another attractive way of serving is in small old-fashioned coffee cups with the spoon in the saucer.

1 large lemon
4 tablespoons fairly sweet
   sherry
2 tablespoons brandy
2 oz caster sugar
½ pint double cream
lemon slices to decorate

1 large lemon
60 ml fairly sweet sherry
30 ml brandy
50 gm caster sugar
300 ml double cream
lemon slices to decorate

Squeeze the juice from the lemon and put in a bowl with the sherry and brandy, add the sugar and stir until dissolved. Pour in the cream and whisk the mixture until it forms soft peaks when the whisk is lifted out. Spoon into individual glasses and leave in a cool place until required. Top each glass with a slice of fresh lemon.

This syllabub may be made a day in advance as it keeps very well. Serves 4.

Barbados cream

A great favourite with many viewers. Yogurt is the ingredient that gives it its beautifully fresh taste.

½ pint double cream
1 pint plain yogurt
soft brown sugar

300 ml double cream
600 ml plain yogurt
soft brown sugar

Lightly whip the cream, blend in the yogurt, turn into a 1½ pint (900 ml) glass dish or 6 small glasses and sprinkle with a ¼ inch (0.60 cm) layer of sugar.

Put in the refrigerator and chill overnight. Sprinkle again with sugar before serving well chilled. Serves 6.

Special ice cream

In my previous family recipe books I have included some of the variations of this ice cream, but here are all the combinations together. It is a superb ice cream, very rich and creamy, and needs no whisking during freezing. This means that the water crystals which appear with French custard-based ice cream are prevented from forming. The ice cream goes into the freezer thick and creamy and just needs to be frozen and solidified.

4 eggs, separated
4 oz caster sugar
½ pint whipping cream
vanilla essence (optional)

4 eggs, separated
100 gm caster sugar
300 ml whipping cream
vanilla essence (optional)

Whisk the yolks in a small bowl until blended. In a larger bowl whisk the egg whites with a hand rotary or electric whisk until stiff. Then whisk in the sugar a teaspoonful at a time. The whites will get stiffer and stiffer as the sugar is added. Blend in the egg yolks until no streaks of colour remain. Whisk the cream until it forms soft peaks and then fold into the mixture and add vanilla essence if liked.

Turn into a 2½ pint (1.4 l) container, cover, label and freeze until frozen solid. Leave to thaw at room temperature for 5 minutes then serve in scoops in small glasses or dishes.

Variations:
(L. to r. Orange chocolate chip, Lemon, Pineapple, Tutti frutti, Fresh mint, Toffee butterscotch.)

Orange chocolate chip: Add about 2 oz (50 gm) crushed chocolate orange sticks to the ice cream before freezing.

Lemon: Use double cream instead of whipping cream. Whisk this with the grated rind and juice of 2 lemons until it forms soft peaks, then fold into the mixture.

Pineapple: Use double cream instead of whipping cream. Cut the flesh from a small pineapple. Add the juice of a small lemon and 2 oz (50 gm) icing sugar.

Puree in a blender then freeze until just set. Fold into the ice cream just before freezing.

Tutti frutti: Add 4 oz (100 gm) chopped glacé cherries, raisins and dried apricots, soaked over-night in 4 tablespoons (60 ml) brandy to plump them up. Fold into the ice cream just before freezing.

Fresh mint: Add a handful of finely chopped mint with a little caster sugar to the ice cream before freezing.

American mint: Add half a bar of crushed seaside rock to the ice cream before freezing. It gives a lovely crunchy taste and speckles the ice cream with pink.

Blackcurrant: Use double cream instead of whipping cream. Add about 6 tablespoons (90 ml) undiluted blackcurrant drink to the cream and fold into the mixture.

Coffee, rum and raisin: Add 2 tablespoons (30 ml) coffee essence and 3 tablespoons (45 ml) rum to about 4 oz (100 gm) chopped, stoned raisins and soak overnight. Fold into the ice cream just before freezing.

Raspberry, strawberry or gooseberry: Use double cream instead of whipping cream. Stir in $\frac{1}{2}$ pint (300 ml) fruit puree to the ice cream just before freezing and add a little colouring if necessary.

Toffee butterscotch: Add about 4 oz (100 gm) crushed butterscotch to the ice cream before freezing.

Cakes and bakes

Grantham gingerbreads

4 oz butter
12 oz caster sugar
1 large egg, beaten
9 oz self-raising flour
1 to 2 level teaspoons
   ground ginger

100 gm butter
350 gm caster sugar
1 large egg, beaten
250 gm self-raising flour
1 to 2 level teaspoons
   ground ginger

These are very good and well worth making. For a variation, the biscuits can be decorated with lemon glacé icing. To 2 teaspoons strained lemon juice beat in sufficient sieved icing sugar to give a fairly stiff icing. Make a greaseproof paper icing bag and fill with the icing. Cut off just the very tip of the bag and pipe a lacy pattern over the tops of the biscuits.

Cream the butter until soft, then beat in the sugar until well blended. Beat in the egg and then add the flour and ginger sieved together (if you like a really gingery taste use 2 teaspoons of ginger) and work to a firm but pliable dough. Knead lightly then roll the dough into balls the size of a walnut. Place well apart on a greased baking sheet. Bake in an oven heated to 300°F, 150°C, Gas No. 2 for 20-30 minutes or until well puffed up and lightly browned. Cool on a wire rack.

N.B. Don't be surprised at the first bite, for these biscuits are hollow in the centre. Makes about 30 biscuits.

Sticky flapjacks

Whilst the oven is on it is always worth making a couple of tins of these flapjacks, as they keep very well. If you haven't two 7 inch (17.5 cm) square tins, you could put all the mixture into a normal-sized roasting tin about 9 inches (22.5 cm) square, provided that the base of the tin is quite flat. Don't be over generous with the golden syrup otherwise the mixture will be too runny.

8 oz margarine
8 oz demerara sugar
2 level tablespoons golden
   syrup
10 oz rolled oats

225 gm margarine
225 gm demerara sugar
2 level tablespoons golden
   syrup
275 gm rolled oats

Grease two 7 inch (17.5 cm) square tins that are about 1½ inches (3.75 cm) deep. Heat the oven at 325°F, 160°C, Gas No. 3.

Melt the margarine in a saucepan, add the sugar and golden syrup and when blended stir in the oats and mix very thoroughly. Divide the mixture between the tins and press down.

Bake in the oven for 25 minutes until just beginning to brown at the edges. Leave to cool for 10 minutes and then mark each tin into 16 squares. Leave in the tin until quite cold, then lift out and store in an airtight tin. Makes 32 flapjacks.

Fruit malt loaf

Very quick to prepare. Weigh all the ingredients straight into the mixing bowl. I haven't left anything out of the ingredients: this recipe really doesn't contain any fat!

6 oz self-raising flour
1 tablespoon malt drink
   (Ovaltine)
1 oz caster sugar
3 oz mixed dried fruit
2 level tablespoons (2 oz or
   50 gm) golden syrup
$\frac{1}{3}$ pint milk

175 gm self-raising flour
1 tablespoon malt drink
    (Ovaltine)
25 gm caster sugar
75 gm mixed dried fruit
2 level tablespoons (50 gm)
    golden syrup
200 ml milk

Mix all the ingredients to a thick batter and put in a 1 lb (450 gm) loaf tin that is well greased. Then bake at 325°F, 160°C, Gas No. 3 for about 1¼ hours until cooked through in the centre. Turn out and leave to cool on a wire rack. Serve sliced with butter.

Chocolate rum truffles

If you would like very potent rum-flavoured truffles, add more rum to the dough and leave it in the refrigerator overnight before rolling into balls.

2 oz seedless raisins,
    chopped
2 oz glacé cherries,
    chopped
4 tablespoons rum
8 oz sweet biscuits,
    crushed
8 oz stale Madeira or
    Victoria sandwich cake,
    crumbled
5 tablespoons drinking
    chocolate
2 tablespoons apricot jam,
    melted
3 oz chocolate vermicelli

50 gm seedless raisins,
    chopped
50 gm glacé cherries,
    chopped
4 tablespoons rum
225 gm sweet biscuits,
    crushed
225 gm stale Madeira or
    Victoria sandwich cake,
    crumbled
5 tablespoons drinking
    chocolate
2 tablespoons apricot jam,
    melted
75 gm chocolate vermicelli

Put the raisins and cherries in a small bowl with the rum and leave to soak for 2 hours. Mix together the crushed biscuits and cake crumbs in a large mixing bowl. Add the drinking chocolate and soaked fruit and mix well, pounding with the back of a wooden spoon. Alternatively use an electric mixer with a dough hook or the beater on a slow speed.

Stir in the melted jam, adding more if necessary to make a firm dough. Shape the dough into small balls and coat them with the chocolate vermicelli by putting them in a polythene bag together and shaking them up. Leave the truffles on a tray or on flat plates to become firm overnight, then place them in small sweet cases. Makes about 48 truffles.

Swiss roll

3 eggs, size 2 at room
temperature
3 oz caster sugar, warmed
3 oz self-raising flour
Filling:
caster sugar
4 tablespoons raspberry jam

3 eggs, size 2 at room
temperature
75 gm caster sugar, warmed
75 gm self-raising flour
Filling:
caster sugar
4 tablespoons raspberry jam

**Swiss rolls are traditionally made
with plain flour, but I find I always
get perfect results with self-raising
flour too. Weigh the ingredients
very accurately and don't over-
whisk the eggs and sugar or you will
have difficulty in folding in the flour
evenly. Roll up the cake as soon as it
comes out of the oven. If it is left to
cool it will crack during rolling.**

Heat the oven to 425°F, 220°C,
Gas No. 7 and grease and line a
Swiss roll tin 9 × 13 inches (22.5
× 32.5 cm) with greased greaseproof paper.

Whisk the eggs and the sugar
together until light and creamy
and the whisk leaves a trail
when lifted out. Sieve the flour
and fold carefully into the
mixture with a metal spoon.
Turn into the prepared tin and
smooth level with the back of
the spoon. Bake in the oven for
about 10 minutes until the
sponge is a golden brown and
begins to shrink from the edges
of the tin.

While the cake is baking cut a
piece of greaseproof paper
slightly bigger than the tin and
sprinkle with caster sugar. Heat
the jam in a small pan until it is
just easy to spread: if it is too hot
it will soak into the cake.

Invert the Swiss roll onto the
sugared paper. Quickly loosen
the paper on the bottom of the
cake and peel off. Trim all four
edges of the sponge and make a
score mark an inch (2.5 cm) in
from the rolling edge, being
careful not to cut right through.
This will make the rolling easier.
Spread with the warm jam, tak-
ing it almost to the edges.

Fold the narrow strip made by
the score mark down onto the
jam and begin rolling, using the
paper to keep a firm and even
roll. Leave the cake for a few
minutes with the paper still
around it to allow it to settle,
and then lift onto a wire cooling
rack. Remove the paper,
sprinkle with a litle more caster
sugar and leave to cool.

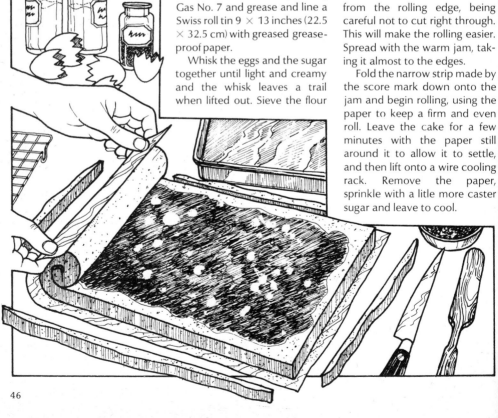

Tray bakes

This is an economical basic recipe made with large families, coffee mornings and bazaars in mind. All the variations are made from one basic mix. Foil tins are ideal if you are making them for sale as the customer can then transport them home more easily.

Put all the ingredients together in a large bowl and mix. Beat well for about 2 minutes. Turn into the prepared tin, greased and lined with greased greaseproof paper, or the foil baking tin. Bake until the cake has shrunk away from the sides of the tin and springs back when pressed with the fingertips at the centre. When the cake has cooled, split, fill with jam and dredge with caster sugar.

For a single quantity baking instructions are as follows: for an 8 inch (20 cm) round tin bake at 350°F, 180°C, Gas No. 4 for 50-60 minutes. For 2 round foil dishes with a top inside measurement of 6½ inches (16.25 cm) bake for 25-30 minutes at the same temperature. For a Bakewell open tart tin 12 × 8 inches (30 × 20 cm) bake at 400°F, 200°C, Gas No. 6 for about 40 minutes.

Bake a double quantity of the mixture in a large meat tin 10 × 12 inches (25 × 30 cm) at 350°F, 180°C, Gas No. 4 for about an hour.

Basic cake mixture:
4 oz soft margarine
6 oz self-raising flour
1 level teaspoon baking powder
4 oz caster sugar
2 eggs, size 3
1-2 tablespoons milk

Basic cake mixture:
100 gm soft margarine
175 gm self-raising flour
1 level teaspoon baking powder
100 gm caster sugar
2 eggs size 3
1–2 tablespoons milk

Variations:

Fruit cake
4 oz (100 gm) currants
1 tablespoon demerara sugar
Add currants to the other ingredients in the mixture and sprinkle the demerara sugar over the cake half way through the cooking time.

Lemon cake
grated rind of 1 lemon

Icing:
juice of 1 lemon
4 oz (100 gm) caster or granulated sugar
Add grated lemon rind to the cake ingredients. When cake comes out of the oven, mix lemon juice and sugar together and spoon over the warm cake.

If the lemon has lots of juice the lemon and sugar mixture will be runny, otherwise it will be more like a sugary paste which has to be spread with the back of a tablespoon over the cake.

Chocolate cake
2 level tablespoons cocoa
2 tablespoons very hot water
Mix cocoa with water to a smooth paste. Cool and add to the ingredients in the cake mixture.

Chococlate icing:
1½ oz (40 gm) margarine
1 oz (25 gm) cocoa, sieved
about 3 tablespoons milk
4 oz (100 gm) icing sugar, sieved
For the icing: melt the margarine in a small pan, stir in the cocoa and cook gently for 1 minute. Remove the pan from the heat and stir in the milk and icing sugar. Mix well to a spreading consistency and spread over the top of the cake.

Bakewell open tart
6 oz (175 gm) shortcrust pastry made with 6 oz (175 gm) flour and 3 oz (75 gm) fat
raspberry jam
½ teaspoon almond essence
flaked almonds
Line a 12 × 8 inch (30 × 20 cm) deepish Swiss roll tin with the pastry and spread with raspberry jam. Top with single quantity basic cake mix with added almond essence and sprinkle with flaked almonds.

Black treacle cake
5 oz (150 gm) black treacle
1 teaspoon mixed spice
icing sugar
Use only 3 oz (75 gm) caster sugar and 2 tablespoons milk , black treacle and mixed spice. Top with a little sieved icing sugar when cool.

Meringues

4 egg whites
8 oz caster or light soft
   brown sugar
double cream

4 egg whites
225 gm caster or light soft
   brown sugar
double cream

Heat the oven to 200°F, 100°C, Gas No. $\frac{1}{4}$ and line 2 baking sheets with silicone paper. Place the egg whites in a large bowl and whisk with an electric or hand rotary whisk until they form soft peaks. Add the sugar a teaspoonful at a time whisking well after each addition until all the sugar has been added. Using 2 dessertspoons, spoon the meringue out onto the baking sheets, putting 12 meringues on each tray.

Bake in the oven for 3 to 4 hours until the meringues are firm and dry and will lift easily from the paper. They will be a very pale off-white and slightly darker if you have used soft brown sugar.

Whisk the cream until thick and use to sandwich the meringue shells together. Makes 12 double meringues.

Chocolate brownies

4 oz self-raising flour
$1\frac{1}{2}$ oz cocoa
4 oz butter
5 oz soft brown sugar
2 eggs, lightly beaten
1 tablespoon milk
Chocolate fudge icing:
$1\frac{1}{2}$ oz butter
1 oz cocoa, sieved
about 3 tablespoons milk
4 oz icing sugar, sieved

100 gm self-raising flour
40 gm cocoa
100 gm butter
150 gm soft brown sugar
2 eggs, lightly beaten
1 tablespoon milk
Chocolate fudge icing:
40 gm butter
25 gm cocoa, sieved
about 3 tablespoons milk
100 gm icing sugar, sieved

Heat the oven to 375°F, 190°C, Gas No. 5 and line with greased greaseproof paper a 7 inch (17.5 cm) square tin, about $1\frac{1}{2}$ inches (3.75 cm) deep. Sieve the flour and cocoa into a bowl.

In another bowl, cream together the butter and sugar until the mixture is light and fluffy. Gradually beat the eggs into the butter mixture, then fold in the sifted flour and cocoa with the milk until well blended. Spoon into the tin and smooth the top.

Bake in the oven for 30 minutes or until the centre of the cake springs back when lightly pressed with a fingertip. Turn the cake out onto a wire rack and leave to cool.

To make the icing: melt the butter in a small pan, stir in the cocoa and cook very gently for one minute. Remove the pan from the heat and stir in the milk and icing sugar. Leave to cool, stirring occasionally until you have a thick spreading consistency. Spread the icing over the cake and leave to set. When quite cold cut into 16 squares. Makes 16 brownies.

Preserves

Quite the most favourite jam with us, the children prefer it to marmalade at breakfast. Pectin is a gum-like substance in fruit which when combined with sugar in jam-making helps the jam to set. Fruits high in pectin such as gooseberries and blackcurrants can take more sugar per lb (450 gm) of fruit. You then get more jam for the amount of fruit used. Fruits low in pectin such as fresh apricots, greengages, plums and raspberries need equal quantities of fruit and sugar. Always choose good quality fruit. It should be under-ripe rather than over-ripe.

Using a copper or brass pan gives the jam a brighter green colour.

I find it best to add commercial pectin, i.e. Certo, to get a good colour, flavour and set to strawberry jam as strawberries are very low in pectin.

Green gooseberry jam

2¼ lb gooseberries
¾ pint water
3 lb granulated sugar

1 kg gooseberries
450 ml water
1. 3 kg granulated sugar

Top and tail the gooseberries. Place them in a large pan with ¾ pint (450 ml) water and bring to the boil. Simmer gently without a lid for about 30 minutes until the mixture is reduced to a pulp and the fruit is soft. At this stage

the contents of the pan will weigh about 2 lb 6 oz (a good kg).

Add the sugar to the pan and stir over a low heat until it has dissolved, then boil rapidly until setting point is reached. This will take about 8 to 10 minutes and can be tested by allowing a teaspoonful to cool on a saucer in the fridge. When pushed with the finger it should ripple.

Pour into clean warm jars and cover with discs of waxed paper. You should either put the tops

on the jars when the jam is still hot or when it is quite cold, then label.

For a variation of the gooseberry jam recipe put 10 heads of elderflowers in a piece of muslin and tie with a string to form a bag. Put this with gooseberries while they are simmering. Before adding the sugar, remove the bag (you will find this easier if you have tied it to the handle of the pan) and squeeze gently using rubber gloves to extract the pectin juice. Makes 5 lb (2.3 kg) jam.

Whole strawberry jam

Hull the fruit and put in a pan with the lemon juice and sugar. Leave to stand for one hour stirring from time to time. Place the pan over a low heat stirring occasionally until the sugar has dissolved. Add a small knob of butter or margarine to reduce foaming. Bring to a full rolling boil and boil rapidly for 4 minutes, stirring occasionally. Remove from the heat and stir in the Certo.

Leave to cool for at least 20 minutes to prevent the fruit floating. Then pour into clean warm jars and cover with a disc of waxed paper. Put the tops on the jars when the jam is quite cold. Label. Makes 5 lb (2.3 kg) jam.

$2\frac{1}{4}$ lb small strawberries
3 tablespoons lemon juice
3 lb sugar
butter or margarine
$\frac{1}{2}$ bottle Certo (commercial pectin)

1 kg small strawberries
45 ml lemon juice
1.3 kg sugar
butter or margarine
$\frac{1}{2}$ bottle Certo (commercial pectin)

Miranda's rhubarb and apple chutney

3 lb apples
$1\frac{1}{2}$ pints malt vinegar
1 lb rhubarb
2 lb soft brown sugar
8 oz chopped dates
8 oz sultanas
1 small red pepper
1 tablespoon ginger powder
2 tablespoons pickling spice, ground
1 teaspoon mixed spice
1 dessertspoon cumin seed
1 teaspoon cayenne pepper
2 tablespoons salt

1. 3 kg apples
900 ml malt vinegar
450 gm rhubarb
900 gm soft brown sugar
225 gm chopped dates
225 gm sultanas
1 small red pepper
1 tablespoon ginger powder
2 tablespoons pickling spice, ground
1 teaspoon mixed spice
1 dessertspoon cumin seed
1 teaspoon cayenne pepper
2 tablespoons salt

Peel, core and roughly chop the apples, place in a pan with half the vinegar and cook to a pulp. Slice the rhubarb into small pieces, place in a large pan with the remaining vinegar and bring to the boil. Simmer for 5 minutes, then add the apple puree, sugar, dates and sultanas. Seed and chop the red pepper and add to the pan with the spices and salt. Bring to the boil and simmer gently for 15-20 minutes until fairly thick and clear looking.

Pour into jars and cover. Store for 2 to 3 months before using. Makes about 8 lb (3.6 kg)

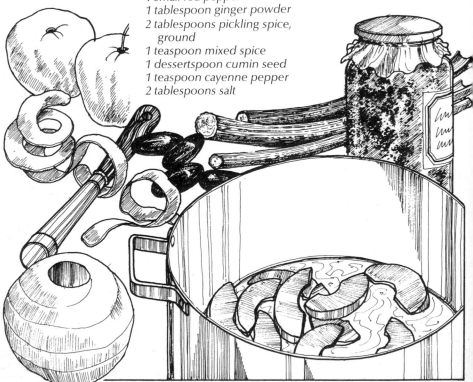

Apple and blackberry jelly

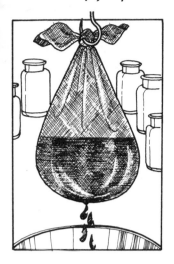

4 lb cooking apples
2 lb blackberries
2 pints water
sugar

1.8 kg cooking apples
900 gm blackberries
1.1 l water
sugar

To test for setting take a scant teaspoon of the jelly and put in a cold saucer. After a few minutes the surface should begin to set and crinkle when pushed with a finger. Do not boil the jelly rapidly while the test is going on, otherwise setting point may be lost. A very good homemade concentrated drink can be made by boiling up the fruit pulp from the bag with 3 pints (1.7 l) of water and 12 oz (350 gm) sugar. Strain and keep in bottles in the refrigerator and dilute to taste with water and ice cubes.

Wash and cut up the apples, removing any bad portions. Wash the blackberries and drain, place in a large pan with the apples and water, cover and simmer until the fruit is a soft pulp. The time will vary with the variety of apples used but will probably be about 30 minutes.

Strain the fruit through a scalded jelly bag and leave overnight. Measure the juice and place in a large pan and bring to the boil. Add the sugar, allowing 1 lb (450 gm) to each pint of juice. Allow the sugar to dissolve and then boil rapidly for 10 minutes. Remove the pan from the heat and test for setting. Skim the jelly, pour at once into warmed jars and cover with waxed circles. Leave to cool. Seal the jars and label and then store in a cool dark place away from strong light. Makes about 3 lb jelly.

Concentrated mint sauce

Making a concentrate like this means that you have mint sauce throughout the winter. Store in a cool place until the season comes round again.

$\frac{1}{4}$ pint malt vinegar
4 oz granulated sugar
1 pint measure finely chopped mint

150 ml malt vinegar
100 gm granulated sugar
600 ml measure finely chopped mint

Pick the mint when it is young and plentiful.

Put the vinegar and sugar in a pan, bring to the boil, stirring until the sugar has dissolved, then boil for one minute. Stir in the mint, remove from the heat and turn into a 1 lb (450 gm) screw-topped jar. Leave to cool, label and store on the larder shelf.

To use, put the required amount in a sauceboat and thin down with a little vinegar and sugar to taste if liked.

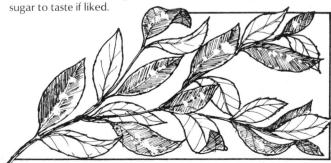

Bread

Garlic rolls

Make garlic bread by the same method as used for Cheese bread rolls, (above). Garlic butter keeps if tightly covered in the refrigerator and is also delicious served on grilled chops and steaks.

2 cloves garlic
a little salt
3 oz butter
freshly ground black pepper
6 crisp white bread rolls

2 cloves garlic
a little salt
75 gm butter
freshly ground black pepper
6 crisp white bread rolls

Peel the garlic and crush to a smooth paste with salt. Cream butter until soft and beat in garlic and black pepper.

Make two cuts an inch (2.5 cm) apart through each roll to within $\frac{1}{2}$ inch (1.25 cm) of the base. Spread with the garlic butter.

Wrap in foil and bake in the oven at 400°F, 200°C, Gas No. 6 for about 15 minutes. Makes 6 rolls.

Cheese bread rolls

These are so easy to make and are ideal to serve with a soup or take on a picnic.

10 oz packet white bread
   mix
6 oz full flavoured Cheddar
   cheese, grated
$\frac{1}{3}$ pint hand-hot water

283 gm packet white bread
*   mix*
175 gm full flavoured
*   Cheddar cheese, grated*
200 ml hand-hot water

Put the bread mix in a bowl with 5 oz (150 gm) of the cheese. Stir in the water and mix together to form a dough. Turn onto a lightly floured table and knead lightly for 5 minutes or until smooth and elastic.

Divide into 8 equal pieces and then shape into rolls, place on a greased baking sheet and inside a large polythene bag and leave in a warm place for about 30-35 minutes or until doubled in bulk.

Whilst the bread is rising, heat the oven to 450°F, 230°C, Gas No. 8.

Sprinkle the remaining cheese over the rolls and bake in the oven for 10 -15 minutes or until well risen and golden brown. Makes 8 rolls.

Quick wheatmeal bread

This bread has only one rising. You first make a yeast liquid and wait until it is frothy, when it is poured onto the other ingredients and mixed together with a fork. Knead until smooth and shape into 4 sausage shapes which are put in a row in the tin to make an interesting shaped loaf.

Rising comes next, followed by baking. For a really crisp loaf lift it out of the tin for the last 10 minutes of cooking.

Yeast mixture:
$\frac{3}{4}$ pint hand-hot water
1 teaspoon sugar
$\frac{1}{2}$ oz dried yeast
Dough:
12 oz strong plain flour
12 oz wholewheat flour
2 teaspoons sugar
2 to 3 teaspoons salt
1 tablespoon salad oil

Yeast mixture:
450 ml hand-hot water
1 teaspoon sugar
12.5 gm dried yeast
Dough:
350 gm strong plain flour
350 gm wholewheat flour
2 teaspoons sugar
2 to 3 teaspoons salt
1 tablespoon salad oil

To make the yeast mixture: mix the water and sugar and stir in the dried yeast. Leave to stand for 10-15 minutes until frothy.

To make the dough: put all the dry ingredients in a bowl. Pour on the yeast mixture and oil and mix with a fork, then knead for about 10 minutes until smooth and no longer sticky.

Grease a 2 lb (900 gm) loaf tin. Take 2 lb (900 gm) in weight of the bread dough and divide into 4 sausage shapes the width of the tin. Lay in the tin and put in a large polythene bag. Shape the remaining dough into 4 bread rolls, place on a small greased baking sheet and put in another polythene bag.

Leave the bread to rise in a cold kitchen for 2 hours or in a warm kitchen for 1 hour, when the rolls will have doubled in bulk and the bread will have risen to the top of the tin.

Bake in the oven at 450°F, 230°C, Gas No. 8. The bread will be evenly browned and sound hollow when tapped on the base after about 40 minutes. The bread rolls will take about 20 minutes.

Salads and dressings

Stuffed tomatoes

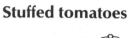

8 large tomatoes
8 oz cream cheese
4 oz cooked ham, very
    finely diced
salt and pepper
1 level tablespoon finely
    chopped chives
watercress to garnish

8 large tomatoes
225 gm cream cheese
100 gm cooked ham, very
    finely diced
salt and pepper
1 level tablespoon finely
    chopped chives
watercress to garnish

Cut a thin slice from the base of each tomato, carefully scoop out the pulp inside and reserve. Cream the cheese with a wooden spoon until it is soft. Mix in the ham and 3 tablespoons of the tomato pulp. Season well and add the chives.

Fill the tomatoes with the cheese and ham mixture and replace the tomato slices on top like a cap.

Arrange on a serving dish and garnish with the watercress. Serve with thinly sliced wholemeal bread. Serves 4.

Coleslaw

1 small, hard white cabbage
   weighing about 1½ lb
½ pint French dressing
salt and pepper
1 level teaspoon Dijon
   mustard
1 small onion, very finely
   chopped
2 carrots
⅛ pint mayonnaise

1 small, hard white cabbage
   weighing about 675 gm
300 ml French dressing
salt and pepper
1 level teaspoon Dijon
   mustard
1 small onion, very finely
   chopped
2 carrots
75 ml mayonnaise

Cut the cabbage into four and trim away any hard stalk, then finely slice into strips. Place in a large mixing bowl with the French dressing, seasoning, mustard and onion, toss well, cover and leave in the refrigerator overnight.

Next day grate the carrots coarsely and stir into the bowl with the mayonnaise. Leave to stand for one hour before turning into a serving dish. Serves 6.

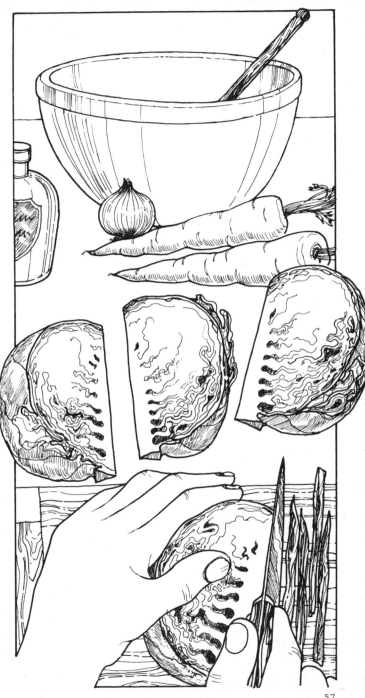

From the top left-hand corner, clockwise: Anchovy mayonnaise, Mint dressing, Tomato cream dressing, Coleslaw, Curry mayonnaise, Tartare sauce, Stuffed tomatoes.

Mayonnaise

2 egg yolks
1 level teaspoon made
  mustard
1 level teaspoon salt
1 level teaspoon caster
  sugar
pepper
1 tablespoon white wine or
  cider vinegar
½ pint corn or vegetable oil
1 tablespoon lemon juice

2 egg yolks
1 level teaspoon made
  mustard
1 level teaspoon salt
1 level teaspoon caster sugar
pepper
1 tablespoon white wine or
  cider vinegar
300 ml corn or vegetable oil
1 tablespoon lemon juice

Should the sauce curdle because the oil has been added too quickly to the egg yolks, take a fresh yolk and start again, adding the curdled mayonnaise very slowly to it in the same way as the oil was added to the original egg yolks.

Stand a bowl on a damp cloth to prevent it slipping on the table. Put yolks, mustard, salt, sugar and pepper into a bowl with the vinegar and mix well. Add the oil drop by drop, beating well with a whisk the whole time until the mixture is smooth and thick. Beat in the lemon juice.

In order that the oil may be added a drop at a time, put into the bottle-neck a cork from which a small wedge has been cut.

Makes ½ pint (300 ml) mayonnaise.

Variations

Curry mayonnaise: Rub the bowl with a cut clove of garlic before starting and then add ½ level teaspoon curry powder to the egg yolk.

Anchovy mayonnaise: Stir 4 teaspoons anchovy essence to the finished mayonnaise and use in fish and vegetable salads.

Herb mayonnaise: Add 1 tablespoon finely chopped parsley, 1 tablespoon finely chopped chives and about 2 tablespoons double cream to the basic recipe and serve with fish or meat salads.

Tartare sauce: To the basic recipe add 1 rounded dessertspoon each chopped gerkins, capers and parsley. Serve with hot fish dishes.

Low-calorie dressing

Well worth making if you're trying to decrease the bulges: it cheers up a salad no end.

1 teaspoon Dijon mustard
1 tablespoon lemon juice
1 tablespoon wine or cider
vinegar
1 crushed clove garlic
5 oz carton plain yogurt
salt and pepper

1 teaspoon Dijon mustard
1 tablespoon lemon juice
1 tablespoon wine or cider
vinegar
1 crushed clove garlic
141 gm carton plain yogurt
salt and pepper

Blend the mustard, lemon juice, vinegar and garlic together in a small bowl, whisk in the yogurt and season well.

Keep covered in the refrigerator and use to dress salads. This dressing will keep for up to 10 days.

Variations

Blue cheese dressing: Add about 1 oz (25 gm) crumbled Roquefort cheese to the dressing and use over a plain green salad. This is especially good when served with plain grilled food such as chops or steaks.

Mint dressing: Add a heaped teaspoon of very finely chopped mint to the basic dressing and mix thoroughly. Use this to dress new potatoes or sliced tomatoes.

Tomato cream dressing: Add a tablespoon tomato ketchup and 2 tablespoons double cream to the basic dressing and serve with fish salads.

Savoury puddings

Suety pudding

2 oz lamb dripping from the roasting tin
4 oz self-raising flour
1½ oz prepared shredded suet
½ level teaspoon salt
1 egg
3 tablespoons milk

50 gm lamb dripping from the roasting tin
100 gm self-raising flour
40 gm prepared shredded suet
½ level teaspoon salt
1 egg
3 tablespoons milk

Heat the oven to 400°F, 200°C, Gas No. 6. Place the dripping in a round shallow ovenproof tin or dish and heat until very hot.

Sift the flour into a basin, stir in the suet and salt. Lightly beat the egg, add with the milk to the mixture and mix to a soft but not sticky dough.

Pat out the dough to the size of the dish on a lightly floured table. Put straight into the hot dripping, return to the oven and cook for about 20 minutes or until golden brown. Cut into wedges and serve with roast lamb. Serves 4.

Herb dumplings

4 oz self-raising flour
2 oz shredded suet
½ level teaspoon salt
1 level tablespoon freshly chopped herbs
about 5-6 tablespoons water

100 gm self raising flour
50 gm shredded suet
½ level teaspoon salt
1 level tablespoon freshly chopped herbs
about 5–6 tablespoons water

Sift the flour into a bowl and stir in the suet, salt and herbs and then mix to a soft but not sticky dough with the water. Form into 8 small balls. Place on top of the casserole or stew, cover and simmer for about 30 minutes until well risen. Serve at once. Makes sufficient dumplings for four people.

Yorkshire pudding

½ oz beef dripping
4 oz flour
1 teaspoon salt
1 egg, lightly beaten
½ pint milk and water mixed

12.5 gm beef dripping
100 gm flour
1 teaspoon salt
1 egg, lightly beaten
300 ml milk and water mixed

Heat the oven to 425°F, 220°C, Gas No. 7. Melt the dripping in a roasting tin 7 × 11 inches (17.5 × 27.5 cm).

Sift the flour and salt into a bowl. Stir in the egg and gradually add the milk and water, mixing to a smooth batter.

Pour into the roasting tin and cook for 35-40 minutes or until the batter is well risen and golden brown and crisp. Serves 4 good portions.

Index

Credits

Artist
Bill McLaughlin
Photographer
John Lee
Home economist
Rosemary Wadey
Cover design
Camron